CALLING ALL SOCIAL WORKERS!

THIS TOTALLY RELATABLE COLORING BOOK WAS MADE JUST FOR YOU

INSIDE THIS BOOK YOU WILL FIND 20 MANDALAS FOR YOU TO SIT BACK AND COLOR

EACH ONE CONTAINS A PROBLEM OR QUOTE THAT YOU SHOULD DEFINITELY BE ABLE TO RELATE TO!

HAPPY COLORING

ISBN-13: 978-1717357878
ISBN-10: 1717357873

COLORING CREW

COLORING CREW

WHEN YOU'RE AT A HOME VISIT AND THEIR PET IS SO DAMN CUTE THAT YOU CAN'T FOCUS

COLORING CREW

COLORING CREW

COLORING CREW

IT ONLY TAKES ONE SOCIAL WORKER TO CHANGE A LIGHTBULB...BUT IT HAS TO WANT TO FUCKING CHANGE

COLORING CREW

COLORING CREW

COLORING CREW

COLORING CREW

COLORING CREW

COLORING
CREW

COLORING CREW

COLORING CREW

A SOCIAL WORKER'S MIND IS LIKE A BROWSER WITH 283 TABS OPEN AT ALL FUCKING TIMES

COLORING CREW

COLORING CREW

I'VE PROBABLY ALREADY SEEN IT, HEARD IT AND WRITTEN A GOAL FOR THAT SHIT

COLORING CREW

COLORING CREW

COLORING CREW

COLORING CREW

THAT MOMENT WHEN YOU REALIZE HOW MANY ASSHOLES ARE WALKING AROUND UNMEDICATED AND UNSUPERVISED

COLORING CREW

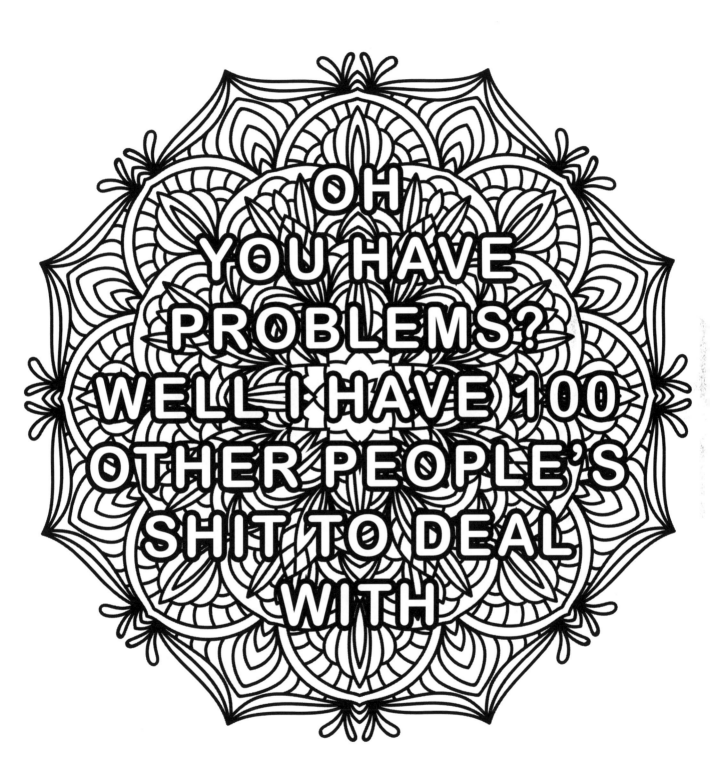

COLORING CREW

COLOR TEST PAGE

COLORING CREW

THANKS!
WE HOPE YOU HAD FUN!

IF YOU LIKED THIS BOOK THEN YOU YOU CAN
VIEW OUR FULL RANGE OF HILARIOUS ADULT
COLORING BOOKS BY GOING TO AMAZON AND
SEARCHING FOR "COLORING CREW" AND THEN
CLICKING ON OUR AUTHOR PAGE.

THANKS AGAIN!

COLORING CREW

Made in the USA
San Bernardino, CA
02 July 2018